D1249501

Module 102-B

Develop Performance Objectives

MODULE 102-B OF CATEGORY B—INSTRUCTIONAL PLANNING
Preparing Better Teachers for Tomorrow (PBTT) Module Series

Center on Education and Training for Employment
The Ohio State University

Initial Development Staff:
    James B. Hamilton, Program Director
    Robert E. Norton, Associate Program Director
    Glenn E. Fardig, Specialist
    Lois B. Harrington, Program Assistant
    Karen M. Quinn, Program Assistant

Revision Staff:
    Robert E. Norton, PBTT Program Director
    Sheri E. Bidwell, Educational Consultant

Copyright © 2001 by the Center on Education and Training for Employment,
The Ohio State University, 1900 Kenny Road, Columbus, Ohio 43210.

Original publication, 1977; Second edition, 1983; Revised, 2001; Second printing 2004

ISBN: 0-89606-361-5

Published and distributed by the
American Association for Vocational Instructional Materials (AAVIM),
220 Smithonia Road, Winterville, Georgia 30683-9527; 1-800-228-4689.

As a career and technical education instructor, you are responsible for helping your students achieve at least entry-level competency in the occupation for which they are preparing. Occupational analyses can reveal what these entry-level competencies are, and courses of study, curriculum guides, and competency profiles can indicate what students should know and be able to do when they leave the program or complete a particular course. However, as you plan the units and lessons that make up the course you are teaching, you will need to be able to translate this information into statements describing the knowledge, skills, and attitudes you want your students to achieve. In other words, you will need to be able to write performance objectives.

In some cases, performance objectives will already have been written for the course you are teaching. In that case, you will, in most cases, be asked to use those performance objectives. Of course, you will need to take into account the needs, interests, and abilities of your particular students as you plan your units and individual lessons.

This module is designed to give you skill in writing clear and measurable performance objectives for your career/technical program that spell out for you, your students, and prospective employers exactly what is expected of students in that program. In addition, it will give you experience in sequencing performance objectives to enhance student learning.

Objectives

Performance Objective:

While working in an actual teaching situation, develop performance objectives. Your performance will be assessed by you and your resource person, using the Performance Assessment Form, pp. 58-59 (*Learning Experience VI*).

Enabling Objectives:

1. Demonstrate knowledge of the rationale for developing performance objectives and the characteristics of properly stated objectives (*Learning Experience I*).
2. Analyze given performance objectives (*Learning Experience II*).
3. Identify each of the objectives on a given list as being primarily cognitive, psychomotor, or affective (*Learning Experience III*).
4. Using resources that provide career/technical program content information, develop performance objectives in each of the learning domains that contain statements of performance, condition, and criterion (*Learning Experience IV*).
5. Sequence a given list of performance objectives. (*Learning Experience V*).

Resources

A list of the outside resources that supplement those contained within the module follows. Check with your resource person to:

- Determine the availability and the location of these resources.
- Locate additional references in your occupational specialty.
- Get assistance in setting up activities with peer(s) or observations of skilled instructors, if necessary.

Your resource person may also be contacted if you have any questions, difficulty with directions, or in assessing your progress at any time.

Learning Experience I
Optional
   Reference: Mager, Robert F. *Preparing Instructional Objectives*. Third Edition. Atlanta, GA: Center for Effective Performance, 1997.
   A *resource person and/or peer(s)* with whom you can meet to discuss or apply the material in the information sheet.
   Resources (e.g., curriculum guides, courses of study, textbooks) in your occupational specialty from which you can obtain performance objectives to critique.

Learning Experience II
Optional
   Reference: Mager, Robert F. *Preparing Instructional Objectives*. Third Edition. Atlanta, GA: Center for Effective Performance, 1997.
   A *resource person and/or peer(s)* with whom you can meet to analyze additional performance objectives.
   Resources (e.g., curriculum guides, courses of study, learning guides. job aids, textbooks) in your occupational specialty from which you can obtain performance objectives to analyze.

Learning Experience III

Optional

    Reference: Armstrong, Robert J. et al. *Developing and Writing Behavioral Objectives.* Tucson, AZ: Educational Innovators Press, 1970.

    Reference: Bloom, Benjamin S. (Ed.). *Taxonomy of Educational Objectives, Handbook I: Cognitive Domain.* New York, NY: Longman, Inc., 1977.

    Reference: Krathwohl, David A., Benjamin S. Bloom, and Bertram B. Masia. *Taxonomy of Educational Objectives, Handbook II: Affective Domain.* New York, NY: Longman, Inc., 1969.

    A *resource person and/or peer(s)* with whom you can discuss the learning domains.

Learning Experience IV

Required

    Resources (e.g., curriculum guides, courses of study, textbooks) in your occupational specialty to provide content from which you can develop performance objectives.

    A *resource person* to evaluate your competency in developing clearly stated performance objectives in each of the learning domains.

Learning Experience V

No outside resources

Learning Experience VI

Required

    An *actual teaching situation* in which you can develop realistic performance objectives.

    A *resource person* to assess your competency in developing performance objectives.

Support Materials

For information about the general organization of each Preparing Better Teachers for Tomorrow (PBTT) module, general procedures for its use, and terminology that is common to all the modules, see About Using the PBTT Modules on the inside back cover. More in-depth information on how to use the modules in teacher/trainer education programs is available in the three documents described below.

These guides were developed for an earlier series of learning modules titled Performance-Based Teacher Education (PBTE). Because the PBTT series is so new, guides that refer specifically to the PBTT modules have not yet been developed. Until they are available, it is recommended that PBTT users refer to the PBTE guides for information about using this module.

The *Student Guide to Using Performance-Based Teacher Education Materials* is designed to help orient preservice and inservice teachers and occupational trainers to PBTE in general and to the PBTE materials.

The *Resource Person Guide to Using Performance-Based Teacher Education Materials* can help prospective resource persons to guide and assist preservice teachers, inservice teachers, and occupational trainers in the development of professional teaching competencies through use of the PBTE modules. It also includes lists of all the module competencies, as well as a listing of the supplementary resources and the addresses where they can be obtained.

The *Guide to the Implementation of Performance-Based Teacher Education* is designed to help those who will administer the PBTE program. It contains answers to implementation questions, possible solutions to problems, and alternative courses of action.

NOTES

Learning Experience I

OVERVIEW

Enabling Objective

Demonstrate knowledge of the rationale for developing performance objectives and the characteristics of properly stated objectives.

Activity 1

You will be reading the information sheet, The Need for Well-Written Performance Objectives, pp. 8-11.

Optional Activity 2

You may wish to read the supplementary reference, Mager, *Preparing Instructional Objectives*, pp. 1-32.

Optional Activity 3

You may wish to meet with your resource person and/or peer(s) to further discuss the information in the reading(s).

Activity 4

You will be demonstrating knowledge of the rationale for developing performance objectives and the characteristics of properly stated objectives by completing the Self-Check, pp. 12-14.

Feedback 5

You will be evaluating your competency by comparing your completed Self-Check with the Model Answers, pp. 16-17.

Activity 1

For information concerning why it is important to develop performance objectives and to state these accurately, read the following information sheet.

THE NEED FOR WELL-WRITTEN PERFORMANCE OBJECTIVES

There once was an instructor who said,
"Writing objectives makes me see red.
I know what to teach
And the students I reach,
So why share what I have in my head?"

To a certain extent the above limerick communicates the feelings that some educators have about performance objectives. There are demands upon all educators, however, to be accountable for the educational process, and upon career and technical educators to be responsive to the needs of the industry for which they are preparing students.

Therefore, it is necessary to **identify the intended outcomes of the educational process**. Performance objectives identify these outcomes.

The need to develop performance objectives can also be viewed from the perspective of the student, the instructor, and the career/technical program.

For **students**, performance objectives provide important information about what is expected of them in the educational program.

- They provide the information students need to determine what the program involves, and describe the activities that they must accomplish in order to complete the program successfully.

- The objectives outline the criteria upon which students' achievement will be measured. Thus, students can determine at any point within the program what they have accomplished and how much remains to be completed.

- If students miss a portion of the program because of illness, they can identify what must be done to complete the missed work.

- If a student has previous experience in a certain area, s/he can determine what objectives s/he has already achieved and work on those objectives that still need to be accomplished.

- Once the expected level of performance has been identified for each objective, the additional experience/practice the students may need in order to reach that level can be outlined.

- There is considerable evidence to indicate that when students know the objectives of the lesson in advance, their motivation and learning is increased.

For **career/technical instructors**, performance objectives provide the necessary blueprint for the instructional process for which s/he is responsible. Performance objectives should define the skills, knowledge, and attitudes necessary for entry into the occupation. It is important to have written performance objectives to keep instructors of the same course on the same track. This is helpful because some instructors tend to stress subject matter and skill development in selected areas within the program based on personal preference rather than occupational requirements. An example of this is a keyboarding instructor who devotes much time and energy on speed-building exercises and little time on other aspects of the program. By basing the objectives on the requirements of the *occupation* for which students are being prepared, instruction can be delivered in an organized fashion and the achievement of the necessary skills can be measured.

In terms of career/technical programs, performance objectives identify for industry those skills that graduates of the program can be expected to possess. Clearly stated performance objectives can give a prospective employer a good idea of what a student coming from your program can do. And, as occupational skills change, the objectives can be changed to match the new expectations.

In addition, the development of performance objectives establishes a base for program evaluation. Questions of whether the graduates will be able to meet the needs of industry can be addressed through the careful examination of how well they are achieving the performance objectives, rather than through the subjective feelings of individuals involved in the evaluation process.

You also need to understand what performance objectives do **not** do. Because performance objectives are written in terms of the student's knowledge, skills, and attitudes, they do not necessarily define the teaching or learning activities that should be used to achieve them. Most performance objectives allow for any number of ways of getting to the final outcome. They define what the outcome must be, but not how to get there.

For example, if a performance objective states that *given leaf samples from diseased trees, the student will identify the diseases with 100% accuracy,* any number of teaching–learning methods might be used in achieving this objective—a field trip to examine diseased trees, presentations with the overhead projector or flip chart, individual or group study. Some students may learn better through studying written materials; others may need to see and handle a diseased leaf in order to be able to identify the disease.

While performance objectives should define the knowledge, skills, and attitudes that **may** be achieved within the career/technical program, they also allow for other relevant experiences and variations. Not **all** of your students should be expected to achieve all the objectives specified for your program, course, or unit. Students learn, and achieve objectives, at different rates. This is one of the reasons that proper sequencing of objectives is essential–so that students, even though they have not achieved all the course objectives, will still have some of the necessary job skills when they leave the program.

Furthermore, some objectives do not state outcomes as specific as those we have been discussing. Yet such objectives have a real place in the career/technical program. These are called expressive or experiential objectives. They describe experiences that would be beneficial for students to participate in, but they do not define expected outcomes. For example, you may feel your students should have the experience of listening to a series of talks by members of community civic organizations, without specifying what changes in behavior they should exhibit as a result.

In general, however, performance objectives define the outcomes of the career/technical program so that these outcomes can be understood by:

- Students, so they can determine exactly what is expected of them.

- Instructors, so they can identify what outcomes they are responsible for.

- Employers and administrators, so they can determine if the program is in fact providing the competent human resources needed.

However, in order for performance objectives to adequately communicate program outcomes, it is essential that the performance be written in such a way that it is **clear** and **measurable**. Certain words commonly used in writing performance objectives are vague and open to several interpretations depending upon who reads the objective and describes the activity outlined. Such words as *know, appreciate,* and *understand* are vague and leave much more room for interpretation than more measurable/observable terms such as *define, describe, repair,* or *analyze*. For example, if you were handed the following objective, would you know what was involved in this activity?

Upon completion of this course, you will know how to repair a computer.

Some of the questions that you would probably ask yourself are:

- Will I have to actually repair the computer or will I only have to describe how it should be done?

- Will I have to locate the problem or will someone else identify the defect so that I can repair it?

- What instruments will I be using?

- What kinds of computers will I "know" how to repair?

As you can see, stating the objectives of an educational program in vague terms requires too much interpretation of what is required of the student. If, instead, you were handed the following objective, would you know what was expected?

Given a non-functioning Pentium IV computer, repair the computer to manufacturer's specifications using the prescribed tools and equipment available in the laboratory.

Objectives that define the behavior or performance in measurable/observable terms (*repair. . .*) are open to less interpretation on the part of the student or instructor. The key to whether the statement is vague or precise is the **verb** (or **action** word) used in the statement. Action-oriented verbs are usually more measurable/observable and less open to varying interpretations. Many reference materials on writing objectives provide lists of action-oriented verbs. Here are some examples:

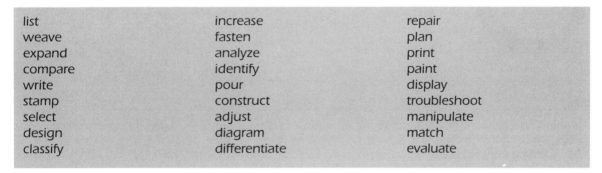

list	increase	repair
weave	fasten	plan
expand	analyze	print
compare	identify	paint
write	pour	display
stamp	construct	troubleshoot
select	adjust	manipulate
design	diagram	match
classify	differentiate	evaluate

Most well-written performance objectives not only specify the **action** to be taken. They also include the **condition** under which the student will be accomplishing the performance (*Given a non-functioning computer...*) and the **criteria** that must be met in order to have successfully completed that objective (*to manufacturer's specifications*).

The information sheet in *Learning Experience II* outlines in more detail what is included in each clearly stated performance objective. At this point, however, it is essential that you be able to recognize a measurable/observable, action-oriented performance statement. The verb will give you the clue.

As you progress through additional modules, you will be writing objectives for various lessons and learning experiences. If you can develop a firm rationale for writing and using objectives, you will find that once they are written, a major part of your instructional planning has been achieved.

For further information on the rationale for developing performance objectives, you may wish to read the supplementary reference, Mager, *Preparing Instructional Objectives*, pp. 1-32.

You may wish to arrange to meet with your resource person and/or peer(s) who are also taking this module. At this meeting you could:

- Discuss what you have heard or read about performance objectives.

- Review existing objectives to determine if they are measurable/observable and action-oriented.

Activity 4

The following items check your comprehension of the material in the information sheet, The Need for Well-Written Performance Objectives, pp. 8-11.

SELF-CHECK

I. Characteristics:

Place a check (✓) by any of the following statements that accurately describe the characteristics of performance objectives. If you do not check a particular statement, briefly explain in writing your reasons for not doing so.

_____ 1. Performance objectives are statements of the general intent of the career/technical program.

_____ 2. Performance objectives provide a basis for evaluating the student, the lesson, and the career/technical program.

_____ 3. Performance objectives outline for instructors how they will teach a particular lesson in the career/technical program.

_____ 4. Performance objectives describe the scope of the program to students, instructors, employers, administrators, parents, and concerned others.

_____ 5. Performance objectives outline what students must achieve in order to exit from the educational program and enter the occupation for which they are preparing.

_____ 6. Performance objectives describe for each student just how they will learn that part of the career/technical program.

II. Rationale:

You have been asked by your school administrator to attend a meeting in which performance objectives will be discussed. In talking with several of the new instructors, you have discovered that they do not see the need for writing performance objectives. On a separate sheet, outline briefly some of the critical points you would make in this meeting to explain to the new instructors why performance objectives lead to more effective learning.

III. Objectives:

Following is a list of partially developed performance objectives that were written by career/technical instructors. Some of these objectives clearly specify the performance desired. In other words, the student would know from the objective exactly what action they were expected to take. Place a check (✓) in front of each statement that clearly specifies the action expected of the student. For any objective that is vague, rewrite the statement to make it accurate and well written.

_____1. Learn the major parts of the internal combustion engine.

_____2. Outline the dietary requirements for an adult female who is moderately active.

_____3. Given a list of terms, you will know all terms listed.

_____4. Upon completion of this course, be aware of the reasons for having clean copy in offset master production.

_____5. Read a blueprint.

_____6. Upon completion of the course in marketing, develop an appreciation of the many people involved in the process of getting goods and services to the public.

_____7. Differentiate among at least three varieties of wheat.

_____8. The student will develop an interest in a health occupations career.

_____9. Given a garment pattern which has any of five different seam types, and the necessary equipment, stitch all of the seams required in that pattern.

_____10. The instructor will motivate the student to learn basic metric measurements.

_____11. After completing the course on basic communication, the student will understand why effective communication is so important.

_____12. Without aid of references, define all terms found in four automobile manufacturers' guides.

_____13. Analyze a given set of tool specifications to determine their appropriateness for replacing brake shoes.

_____14. Adjust the gap of spark plugs to within .003 of manufacturer's specifications.

_____15. Given a list of performance statements, check (✓) those that are action-oriented (clearly written).

Compare your written responses on the Self-Check with the Model Answers given below. For parts I and III, you should have checked the same statements as those checked in the model responses. For parts I and II, your written responses need not exactly duplicate the model responses; however, you should have covered the same major points. For part III, your rewritten statements should closely match the model responses.

MODEL ANSWERS

I. Characteristics:

_____ 1. Performance objectives oriented statements which describe what the student will be achieving within a given lesson. They are not general in nature, but very **specific** in outlining student action and measurement of student performance.

___✓__ 2.

_____ 3. Performance objectives are written in terms of **student performance**. Therefore, the instructor must select the most appropriate activities to assist the student in achieving a particular objective.

___✓__ 4.

___✓__ 5.

_____ 6. Performance objectives outline the **outcome** of the learning, but do not necessarily identify how that learning will take place. Students often have some options available to them, the choice of which depends on their own learning style.

II. Rationale:

Answers will vary; however, you should have covered the following points:

1. **The importance to the student**; e.g., performance objectives outline what is required of them to complete the career/technical program.

2. **The importance to the instructor**; e.g., performance objectives define what skills, knowledge, and attitudes they will be responsible for helping students acquire.

3. **The importance to the career/technical program**; e.g., performance objectives outline for employers and concerned others what can be expected of graduates, and provide the basis for program evaluation.

4. The fact that **performance objectives outline the required outcomes of the career/technical program** so that students, instructors, and others know what achievements can be expected.

III. Objectives:

_____ 1. Learn is an action-oriented word; however, it is not precise.
Restated: *Name (identify, point out) major parts of the internal combustion engine.*

__✓__ 2.

_____ 3. *Know* is open to interpretation. Are the students simply to memorize the list or is something more required?
Restated: *Define (match with definitions, describe) terms in a given list.*

_____ 4. The term *aware of* does not outline what the student will be doing.
Restated: *List (explain) the reasons for having clean copy in offset master production.*

__✓__ 5.

_____ 6. What is meant by *appreciation?* An action verb should have been used.
Restated: *... list the people involved in the process of..., or ... trace an item from producer to consumer.*

__✓__ 7.

_____ 8. What does *develop an interest* mean exactly? How could the development of this interest be measured?
Restated: *Choose one of the five health careers available within the cluster; or List seven health careers in which s/he is interested.*

__✓__ 9.

_____ 10. This statement is instructor-related, and it is not action-oriented. It should be student-oriented and contain an action verb.
Restated: *...convert a given list of English measures to metric measures.*

_____ 11. *Understand* is one of those terms which leaves much room for interpretation.
Restated: *Explain why a given piece of communication is effective or ineffective; or List (describe) at least three problems which may arise when basic communication breaks down.*

__✓__ 12.

__✓__ 13.

__✓__ 14.

__✓__ 15.

LEVEL OF PERFORMANCE: For parts I and III, your checked items should exactly duplicate the model responses. For parts I and II, your written responses should have covered the same major points. For part III, your rewritten statements should closely match the model responses. If you missed some points or have questions about any additional points you made, review the material in the information sheet, *The Need for Well-Written Performance Objectives*, pp. 8-11, or check with your resource person if necessary.

NOTES

OVERVIEW

Enabling Objective

Analyze given performance objectives.

Activity 1

You will be reading the information sheet, The Components of a Clearly Written Performance Objective, pp. 20-26.

Optional Activity 2

You may wish to read the supplementary reference, Mager, Preparing Instructional Objectives, pp. 43-82.

Activity 3

You will be analyzing and (if necessary) rewriting given performance objectives by completing the Analysis Form, pp. 27-29.

Feedback 4

You will be evaluating your competency in analyzing and rewriting objectives by comparing your completed Analysis Form with the Model Analysis, pp. 30-31.

Optional Activity 5

You may wish to meet with your resource person and/or peer(s) to review and analyze additional performance objectives in your occupational specialty.

For information concerning the components of a clearly written performance objective, read the following information sheet.

THE COMPONENTS OF A CLEARLY WRITTEN PERFORMANCE OBJECTIVE

One of the potentially confusing things about writing objectives is that the term *objective* is used in so many different contexts. In the educational program, objectives are written for the overall educational program, for a specific course, for units of instruction, for learning packages, and for individual lessons. In addition, the word *objective* is used in program evaluation and management contexts to describe what the instructor (or worker) should accomplish during a specific period of time in relation to a group of students or other people. Some individuals use the term *objective* inappropriately to describe broad program goals or the general intent of the educational program. To a certain extent, this variety of usage is understandable in that the word *objective*, by definition, means an end of action.

Another source of confusion results from the fact that authors, in defining what components need to be included in a clearly stated objective, use different terminology for these components.

Throughout this module and in other modules, we use the term *performance objective*, which refers to an action-oriented statement describing what is to be achieved by the students of a career/technical program.

Performance Objectives

1. **Performance**
2. **Condition**
3. **Criterion**

The form of performance objective statement described in this module includes three components: **performance**, **condition**, and **criterion**. This form was developed by Mager and is widely accepted. It should be pointed out, however, that some competency-based programs and materials do not include the criterion and/or condition components as part of the objective statement because they have other well-organized ways of dealing with these important components.

Performance Component

The **performance** part of an objective describes what the student will be *doing*. It must contain an **action verb**. Each of the enabling objectives contained in this module describes the performance to be achieved using an action-oriented verb (underlined below).

- <u>Demonstrate</u> knowledge of the rationale for developing performance objectives and the characteristics of properly stated objectives.

- <u>Analyze</u> given performance objectives.

- <u>Identify</u> each of the objectives on a given list as being primarily cognitive, psychomotor, or affective.

- <u>Develop</u> performance objectives in each of the learning domains that contain statements of performance, condition, and criterion.

- <u>Sequence</u> a given list of performance objectives.

The terms *action required* and *activity* also have been used to describe this component.

Condition Component

The condition part of the objective outlines the circumstances under which the student will be required to perform the activity. This portion of the objective can describe:

- What equipment, supplies, or materials the student will be given to work with.

- What materials the student will be denied access to.

- What setting the performance must be demonstrated in.

- What information the student may be provided that will direct the action in a certain way.

- What amount of time will be allowed for the performance to be accomplished.

Sample 1, p. 22, shows some examples of conditions that might be included within each of these general categories. Stating the condition as *upon completion of the unit* may be convenient but it ignores the actual, specific circumstances under which the student will be performing a particular activity. Hence, such condition statements may be neither accurate nor helpful.

Another word that has been used to describe this components is *givens*.

Criterion Component

The criterion part of the performance objective describes the level of mastery or degree of proficiency that must be reached in carrying out the performance; in other words, how well the student must be able to do the job. The criterion tells the student (and instructor) what level of performance is required in order for the performance objective to be achieved.

This part of the objective is probably the most difficult to write, but once done, it also provides information necessary for planning how to evaluate performance. There are several ways in which the criterion may be established, including one or more of the following:

- Accuracy within a tolerance limit

- Speed

- Percent or number to be achieved

- Reference to other material that identifies specific criteria (e.g., performance checklist)

- Maximum number of permissible errors

- Degree of excellence

Sample 2, pp. 23-24, shows some examples of criteria that might be included within each of these general categories.

CONDITION STATEMENTS

CATEGORY	EXAMPLES OF CONDITIONS
Equipment, supplies, or materials the student is given to work with	<ul><li>Using equipment available in the electronics laboratory</li><li>Given a set of blueprints</li><li>Provided access to all reference and materials in the DE store</li><li>Given a list of performance objectives</li><li>Using curriculum guides that provide program content information</li></ul>
Materials to which the student will be denied access	<ul><li>Without aid of references</li><li>Using only those materials provided</li><li>Using only that equipment that has been set up</li></ul>
Environment in which the performance must be demonstrated	<ul><li>In an actual teaching situation</li><li>In a simulated classroom or laboratory situation</li><li>While in the hospital or nursing home</li><li>Using the auto mechanics laboratory</li></ul>
Information that the student may be provided that will direct the action in a certain direction	<ul><li>Given a written situation involving a family with ethnic eating patterns</li><li>Provided two lists—one of terms and another of definitions</li><li>Using a case study provided by the instructor</li><li>Upon completion of the course in sales</li></ul>

CRITERION STATEMENTS

GENERAL CATEGORY	EXAMPLES OF CRITERION
Accuracy within a tolerance limit	• Within ± .1 degree as compared with the instructor's reading
	• With a tolerance of ± .001 inch as measured by a micrometer
Speed	• Completed within five minutes
	• Ready for return to the customer within 24 hours of drop-off
Percent or number to be achieved	• With 80% correct responses
	• Two out of the three items must meet criteria for the finished product
	• All information necessary for a dental history is recorded
	• At the rate of five per hour
Reference to other material that identifies specific criteria	• As compared to the manufacturer's specifications
	• Using the evaluation guide that outlines specific criteria for table setting
	• According to the criteria outlined in the text
	• According to written office procedures
	• Based upon the criteria specified in the assessment instrument
Maximum number of permissible errors	• With no more than two errors
	• With no more than one total item not meeting the stated standards
	• Missing no more than one reading/recording within a two hour period

Degree of excellence	
	▪ Such that the seam will not split when the two pieces of material are jerked sharply
	▪ So that when the weld is submitted to a stress machine it will withstand 100 pounds of pressure
	▪ All criteria must be achieved at the good or excellent level
	▪ With no hair visible in the operating field
Or any combination	▪ The above criteria can be combined to further define the level of achievement necessary.

As you can see in Sample 2, the criterion may be stated in many ways—as long as it specifies a realistic level to be achieved. As in writing conditions, there is a quick way of defining criteria: *with 80% correct.* This is **not** an appropriate criterion in most cases, however. The level of performance required should be based on specific criteria relating to a particular performance under particular conditions, rather than on an arbitrary percentage.

"Aha!" you say, "There are those educators again telling us what to do and not doing it themselves. This module's enabling objectives do not include criterion statements. You are right in that the enabling objectives, as they appear in the Overviews, do not define the criteria for achievement.

However, the criterion for each objective is defined in the feedback activity in each learning experience. It is possible to provide criterion other than within the performance objective statement itself...if you let students know where they can find the necessary information describing the level that must be achieved. Note: In this module, an explicit list of performance criteria is included in the Performance Assessment form, p. 58-59.

Until you have gained experience in writing objectives, however, it is suggested that you include the criterion within the performance objective statement. Once you are thoroughly competent in writing performance objectives, you will find that there are many ways that clear and complete objectives can be written without including all components within a single statement. Other words that have been used to describe this component are *mastery level* or *standard.*

Complete Statements

Each of these three components should be present in a clearly stated performance objective. Let's take a look at some performance objectives and examine these components in more detail. See if you can identify the performance, condition, and criterion for the following performance objectives:

> *Given a case situation involving a family with ethnic eating patterns, and the necessary meal planning guides, plan a balanced diet for that family that will meet basic nutritional standards and take into account the family's eating patterns.*

You should have identified the condition as...*Given a case situation involving a family with ethnic eating patterns and the necessary meal planning guides...*You should have identified the performance as ...*plan a balanced diet for a family...*, and the criterion as ...*that will meet basic nutritional standards and take into account the family's eating pattern.*

This is a rather involved performance objective. The condition includes two different items and the criterion includes two different items to consider in determining whether the student has achieved the objective. What about the next objective—can you identify the components?

Upon completion of the unit in basic architectural drafting, make working drawings of any of the designs covered in class with 100% accuracy.

This objective contains all the components of a clearly stated objective, but does the objective really tell the students under what conditions they will be *drawing*? What does the 100% mean? It really isn't enough to write performance objectives that contain all of the necessary components if they are misleading for the instructor or student.

The student should be given specifications to work from, along with the necessary drafting tools and material. The criterion for acceptable performance should outline the specific characteristics the finished drawings must have or refer the student to an established set of criteria. A more realistic objective might be stated as follows:

Given a set of building specifications for any of the basic designs covered in class, make a set of working drawings of that building using any materials/supplies needed so that the drawings contain all of the characteristics outlined in the evaluation sheet.

This is a realistic objective to be used in judging the finished drawings. Since this objective would probably be completed toward the end of the unit, it would not be efficient to list all of the criteria to be considered. You would, however, need to provide the students access to, or copies of, the evaluation sheet that would outline the specific criteria to be met by the completed drawings.

Enabling Objectives

In most curriculum development efforts, two or more enabling objectives are written to support achievement of the performance objective. As the *enabler* term implies, the enabling objectives help the learner achieve the performance objective. Usually the first one or two enabling objectives focus the learner on gaining the *knowledge* needed, while the second or third enabling objective focuses on providing opportunities for the learner to *practice*. Enabling objectives may also be written to include both knowledge and practice in the same learning experience.

Typically, each enabling objective is associated with a specific learning experience in a module, learning guide, or other type of learning package. The learning experience will consist of a series of sequenced learning activities designed to help the learner achieve that portion of the performance objective.

A sample competency and its associated performance objective and enabling objectives follow.

Competency: Perform Wheel Alignment

Performance Objective:

Given the need to maintain the proper operation of the steering system, perform wheel alignment. Your performance must meet the criteria for wheel alignment procedures as noted on the Performance Test.

Enabling Objectives:

1. *Gain knowledge* of wheel alignment principles.
2. *Practice recognizing* proper and improper wheel alignment.
3. *Practice performing* wheel alignment procedures.

LEVEL OF OBJECTIVES

Course Objective	Upon completion of the general surgical procedures course, function as first scrub in any routine abdominal or peritoneal cases. Evaluation will be done by the supervisory nurse, using clinical evaluation forms.
Unit Objective	Assigned any of the routine abdominal cases in the operating room, prepare suture, needles, and other supplies for that case and doctor using preference cards. The instructor will check your selection against the cards and procedures.
Lesson Objective	List differences between first and second scrub responsibilities. Your list should match the list presented in class. OR Given the necessary equipment and supplies for major surgery, set up the back table for the procedure according to clinical procedure and without contamination.

Level of Specificity Required

The level of specificity required of good performance objectives depends, in part, on the level for which they are being written. One of the criticisms of performance objectives has been that they are often too specific. In many cases, objectives written for **lesson plans** or **learning packages** are very specific because they cover only a small part of the educational program. However, performance objectives written for **units** or **courses** are usually much broader in scope, covering a wider range within the educational program. Sample 3 shows an example of a sequence of performance objectives that might be developed for an operating-room technician program.

As you can see in Sample 3, each of these performance objectives contains the necessary components of a clearly stated objective, but there is quite a difference in the scope that each objective covers. In later modules, you will be developing units of instruction and lesson plans that will require you to write performance objectives. Depending on the scope of the plan, you will need to judge how specific the objective must be to be appropriate.

No matter when the objective is to be achieved, however, it must contain statements of the performance to be achieved, conditions under that the learner will be working and the level that must be achieved in order to satisfactorily accomplish that objective.

If you have some questions about the component parts of a clearly stated performance objective, you may wish to read the supplementary reference, Mager, *Preparing Instructional Objectives*, pp. 43-82. This reference provides some exercises for you to complete to help you recognize and develop clearly stated objectives.

The following activity checks your ability to identify the components of a clearly stated performance objective. The list below contains statements that may or may not contain all the components of clearly state student performance objectives. Examine each statement and do the following:

1. Circle the performance.

2. Underline the condition with one line.

3. Underline the criterion with two lines.

4. Rewrite any objective that does not contain all three components and/or that contains a component that is vague, inappropriate, or unrealistic. Briefly explain why you rewrote the objective.

ANALYSIS FORM

1. Grease all critical points outlined by the manufacturer on any automobile coming into the laboratory requiring routine maintenance.

2. Given sample résumés, learn how to write one of your own.

3. Stitch any of the heavy material garments in such a way that they will pass simulated inspection guidelines.

4. Calculate the missing value on 80% of the Ohm's law problems that will outline any two of the values for current, voltage, or resistance.

5. Using the form provided, critique each of the sales presentations within one-half hour.

6. Given examples of completed auto repair forms, price the work using any of the price lists.

7. Outline optimum storage requirements for any of the foods in a given list.

8. In an actual teaching situation, write performance objectives for a career/technical lesson. Your performance will be assessed by your resource person, using the Performance Assessment Form.

9. Given ten thermometers registering different temperatures, read each thermometer with 100% accuracy.

10. Prepare a soil mixture for potting plants that contains the recommended amounts of each ingredient; the size of the particles should be no more than $1/_8$ inch in diameter.

Compare your completed written Analysis Form with the Model Analysis given below. Your analysis of the performance objectives as to performance, condition, and criteria should exactly match the model responses. Your rewritten objectives should contain all three components, clearly stated as suggested in the model objectives. Your explanations need not exactly duplicate the model responses; however, you should have covered the same major points.

MODEL ANALYSIS

1. **Performance:** grease (car parts)
   Condition: on any automobile coming into the laboratory requiring routine maintenance
   Criterion: all critical points outlined by the manufacturer

2. **Performance:** learn how to write your own
   Condition: given sample résumés

   This objective does not contain either a measurable/observable statement of performance (*learn how* is vague) or a criterion. It could be written as follows:

   Given sample résumés, develop your own résumé that contains all essential elements as identified in the samples.

3. **Performance:** stitch any of the heavy material garments
   Criterion: in such a way that they will pass simulated inspection guidelines

   This objective does not contain the conditions under which the student will be performing. It could be rewritten as follows:

   Given cut pieces of heavy material garments and the necessary patterns, stitch any of the heavy material garments in such a way that they will pass simulated inspection guidelines.

4. **Performance:** calculate the missing value of the Ohm's law problems
   Condition: which will outline any two of the values for current voltage or resistance
   Criterion: on 80%

5. **Performance:** critique a sales presentation
   Condition: using the form provided
   Criterion: within one-half hour

   This objective does not contain a measurable/observable statement of the conditions under which students will be critiquing. They are told they will be given a form to use, but not whether they will be critiquing a live sales presentation, videotaped presentation, or simulated classroom presentation. In addition, the criterion as stated (within one-half hour) is not really appropriate. The speed with which the critique is done is not as important as the accuracy of the critique. The objective could be rewritten as follows:

   After viewing a videotaped sales presentation, critique the presentation, using the critique form provided. Your critique must match the model critique.

6. **Performance:** price the work
   Condition: given examples of completed auto repair forms; using any of the price lists.

This objective does not contain a criterion. How well must the work be priced? This objective could be rewritten as follows:

Given examples of completed auto repair forms, price the work, using any of the price lists, with no more than $1.00 error in ten tabulations.

7. **Performance:** outline storage requirements
   Condition: for any of the foods in a given list
   Criterion: optimum

   If the optimum requirements have been defined previously, and the students know where this information is to be found (e.g., handout, reference material), then this objective is complete. However, the specific guidelines (criterion) could have been mentioned in the objective.

8. **Performance:** write performance objectives for a career/technical lesson
   Condition: in an actual teaching situation
   Criterion: your performance will be assessed by your resource person, using the Performance Assessment Form.

9. **Performance:** read each thermometer
   Condition: given ten thermometers registering different temperatures
   Criterion: with 100% accuracy

   This objective is complete. However, you may have questioned the appropriateness of the criterion (with 100% accuracy). ± 1 degree might be more realistic.

10. **Performance:** prepare a soil mixture for potting plants
    Criterion: which contains the recommended amounts of each ingredient; the size of the particles should be no more than $1/_8$ inch in diameter

    This objective does not contain a statement of the conditions under which students will be working. What will they be given to work with? This objective could be rewritten as follows:

    Using the soil (materials) available in the horticulture room, prepare a soil mixture for potting plants that contains the recommended amounts of each ingredient; the size of the particles should be no more than $1/_8$ inch in diameter.

LEVEL OF PERFORMANCE: Your analysis of the objectives should have been the same as the model responses. Your rewritten objectives should contain all three components and be clearly and accurately stated. Your explanations should cover the same major points as the model objectives. If you missed some points or have questions about any additional points you made, review the material in the information sheet, The Components of a Clearly Written Performance Objective, pp. 20-26, or check with your resource person if necessary.

You may wish to meet with your resource person and/or other peer(s) taking this module to review a list of performance objectives in your occupational specialty and use the keying symbols from the Analysis Form, pp. 27-29, to analyze these objectives. Your resource person can help you find objectives, and most curriculum guides in your occupational speciality will contain objectives you can use.

NOTES

OVERVIEW

Enabling Objective

Identify each of the objectives on a given list as being primarily cognitive, psychomotor, or affective.

Activity 1

You will be reading the information sheet, Performance Objective Domains, pp. 34-41.

Optional Activity 2

You may wish to read the supplementary references, Bloom, *Taxonomy of Educational Objectives, Handbook I: Cognitive Domain*; and/or Krathwohl, *Taxonomy of Educational Objectives, Handbook II: Affective Domain*.

Optional Activity 3

You may wish to meet with your resource person and/or peer(s) to discuss the reading(s) or to further clarify which performances in your occupational area would be included in each of the domains.

Activity 4

You will be identifying performance objectives as being primarily cognitive, psychomotor, or affective by completing the Domain Identification Form, pp. 43-44.

Feedback 5

You will be evaluating your competency in identifying the domains in which each of the performance objectives belong by comparing your completed Domain Identification Form with the Model Identification Form, p. 46.

Optional Activity 6

You may wish to identify the general taxonomic level of each objective.

Activity 1 For information about the domains of performance objectives and the taxonomic levels within each domain, read the following information sheet.

PERFORMANCE OBJECTIVE DOMAINS

Another dimension of writing performance objectives is the different types of performances that can be specified. Just as your own behavior patterns are made up of different types of activities, so are the objectives that must be achieved so that students leave a program and go into the occupation for which they are being prepared.

These activities include *knowing* certain information (classified as the cognitive domain), performing certain physical *skills* (classified as the psychomotor domain), and exhibiting certain *personal qualities, feelings, or attitudes* (classified as the affective domain).

As an instructor, you will need to be able to develop objectives that emphasize the cognitive, psychomotor, and/or affective domains. Each of these domains has certain characteristics. Let's take a detailed look at each domain and at some of the performances, conditions, and criteria that might be appropriate for each.

Cognitive Domain

The cognitive domain includes those **performances** that require *knowledge* of specific information; e.g., the principles, concepts, and generalizations necessary for problem solving. The following are examples of cognitive performances:

- *Define the terms*

- *Critique the presentation*

- *Develop your resume*

- *Identify given objectives as being primarily cognitive, psychomotor, or affective*

Conditions (circumstances under which such performances would be accomplished) could be any situation in which the student is given information to process, such as:

- *Given a list of terms*

- *After viewing videotaped lesson presentations*

- *Given sample resumes*

- *Given a list of performance objectives*

Criteria within the cognitive domain will usually call for accuracy of the information to a certain standard, or will make reference to other material. These could include:

- *With 80% correct responses*

- *According to the model answers*

- *Compared to a model*

Psychomotor Domain

The psychomotor domain measures the **skill** performance of the student and, therefore, the performance required usually will involve the manipulation of objects, tools, supplies, or equipment. Performances that are primarily psychomotor include the following:

- *Typing a letter*

- *Constructing a wall*

- *Wiring a plug*

- *Developing an x-ray*

- *Writing a computer program*

- *Operating a calculator*

- *Coloring hair*

Since students will be manipulating something such as tools, equipment, supplies, or machinery, the **conditions** for the psychomotor objective will need to describe the necessary materials or environment, such as the following:

- *In a simulated office situation*

- *Given the necessary blueprints and construction materials*

- *For any non-functioning computer brought into the shop*

- *Following film exposure*

- *For any field with no more than 5° slope*

Similarly, the **criterion** for the achievement of a psychomotor objective will relate to the actual performance or the finished product and to the necessary level of performance that must be achieved. Appropriate criteria for objectives in the psychomotor domain might involve accuracy within a certain tolerance limit, speed, degree of excellence, or reference to other material outlining the criteria for judgement. Examples of such criteria might include the following:

- *At 50 words per minute with no more than two errors*

- *So that the wall meets the criteria specified within the blueprint and will pass inspection using the Wall Construction Criteria Checklist*

- *According to manufacturer's specifications*

- *To a .001 inch tolerance as measured by a micrometer*

- *According to the procedure outlined in the manufacturer's manual*

- *So that the shine will reflect a piece of paper*

Affective Domain

In the affective domain the **performance** required involves the demonstration of feelings, behaviors, attitudes, or sensitivities toward other people, ideas, or things. For example, the student might be asked to do the following:

- *Demonstrate an increased awareness*

- *Show concern for safety within the laboratory*

- *Display a concerned attitude toward frightened patients*

- *Take responsibility for his/her learning*

The **conditions** under which these feelings, behaviors, or attitudes will be demonstrated are situations in which students can demonstrate beginning understandings of the necessary worker behaviors required in the occupation. Examples of condition statements might include the following:

- *Upon completion of the unit on personnel relations*

- *At all times within the laboratory*

- *In the actual work situation*

In the affective domain, since feelings are not directly measurable, the **criterion** for achievement of an objective calls for behavior that demonstrates that a feeling or attitude is present. Therefore, both the criterion and the performance statement will contain an action word or verb. Examples of such criteria follow:

- *Stays with an apprehensive patient during examination*

- *Reports a hazardous condition in the laboratory*

- *Participates in class discussion voluntarily*

- *Greets customers upon arrival*

You may have heard that objectives within the affective domain are difficult to write because feelings and attitudes are not easy to measure. One of the reasons that objectives in the affective domain are difficult to measure is that people show feelings and attitudes in many different ways. Think of a point in your life when you were upset about something. Did all of your friends and acquaintances react to your unsettled condition in the same way? Probably some asked you outright what was wrong. Other may not have asked, but made themselves available to you when you were ready to talk about the problem. Still others may have indicated to you in other ways that they realized you were upset, but would wait for you to take the initiative in making your feelings known.

Similarly, we do not expect all students to exhibit the same behavior in demonstrating the necessary attitudes for an occupation. Rather, the career/technical instructor is more concerned that all students can function appropriately, based on their own individuality, in the actual work situation. As you begin to write affective objectives, ask yourself the following questions:

1. *Are these feelings or attitudes that are really required at entry level by the industry for which I am preparing my students or are these attitudes I feel the students should possess?*

2. *If I were watching students who possessed this feeling or attitude, what type of behavior might I expect them to exhibit?*

In many cases the answer to the first question will be that the instructor is making unrealistic demands in terms of actual entry-level requirements.

In answering the second question, think about the behavior patterns you might expect in a particular situation; e.g., how do employees who respect their co-workers behave in the work situation? Then, provide a variety of options for students to demonstrate, in their own way, that they have the necessary attitudes and feelings to exhibit the desired behavior.

Selecting the Domain

It should be noted that few objectives are *purely* cognitive, psychomotor, or affective. The major criterion in determining the domain in which an objective belongs is the **primary** performance called for–if it relates primarily to **knowing** about the subject, it is cognitive; if it relates primarily to **skill** development, it is psychomotor; and if it relates primarily to **feelings/attitudes**, it is affective.

Taxonomic Levels

Different performances have been identified as being primarily cognitive, psychomotor, or affective, but there are also **levels** within each of these domains that move from very simple performances to the more complex. These levels taken as a whole are termed a *taxonomy.*

The taxonomy in the cognitive domain moves from the lowest level of knowledge (that of simple remembering or recall) to the more complicated thinking processes required for evaluation. Sample 4 shows the differing levels within the cognitive domain. As you will note, each of the higher levels within the chart requires that the lower levels be met first in order for the higher level to be accomplished. In other words, in order to reach the application level (i.e., to apply knowledge), the student must first possess the basic knowledge and also comprehend it.

Similarly, the levels within the psychomotor domain progress from simple skills to complex skill development in which several tasks are integrated into a coordinated whole. In one taxonomy, the more complex motor skill is developed through stages—from the imitation of a model to the point at which performance of the skill becomes automatic or habitual. Sample 5 illustrates this development. As you can see, each successive level within the domain requires more complicated forms of psychomotor skills and/or a combination of several skills into a coordinated sequence.

The affective domain also includes levels, but instead of the development from simple to complex found in the cognitive and psychomotor domains, each succeeding level involves more

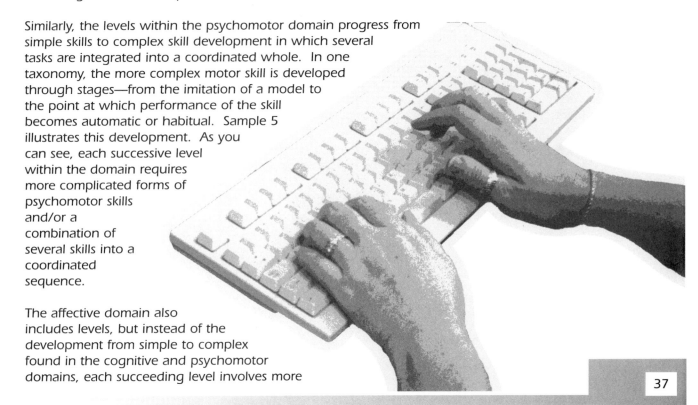

internalization of the feeling or attitude; i.e., the behavior becomes a part of the student's or worker's total way of responding. In the lower levels of the domain, therefore, the student is simply provided the necessary information so as to know what an appropriate response is, and is only required to passively attend (be aware of) that information. The highest level within the affective domain is achieved when the student or worker has *internalized* the information. Sample 6 outlines the development within the affective domain.

The taxonomies within the cognitive, psychomotor, and affective domains provide a *method* by which career/technical instructors can organize or sequence the objectives for their particular instructional units and lessons. By identifying the domain in which the objective belongs and the taxonomic level of the objective, it is possible to develop instruction in such a way that lower-level objectives within each of the domains are achieved before the student progresses to higher-level ones. In most cases, the higher-level objectives will be reached toward the end of a particular unit or toward the end of the career/technical program.

One word of caution: It may not be possible or desirable within the time frame of your career/technical program to develop all cognitive, psychomotor, or affective objectives through the highest level of each domain. For example, some of the very early motor skills may be developed to a naturalization level (done automatically and with ease), but it would not be possible or even realistic to expect all skills to be developed to this level. Similarly, in the affective domain it may not be possible within a career/technical program to proceed beyond the valuing level because of the time limits of the program. Furthermore, it may not be appropriate to expect students to develop certain feelings or attitudes beyond valuing them (behaving) appropriately in the work situation.

In all cases, the key as to what level is necessary within your career/technical program is the level required by the industry for which you are preparing students. You may only be able to prepare your students to respond in the appropriate manner; the industry would then take over so that over a much longer period of time the behavior becomes a consistent and internalized response. This is one of the reasons that developing objectives is a time consuming task. Not only do you have to be able to write the objectives, but you must ask yourself whether these objectives are appropriate for the level of the program offered and the students entering it.

In order to define the career/technical program so that the students will be able to leave the program and enter the occupation for which they are preparing, objectives should be written in all domains. Knowledge of information is necessary; therefore, cognitive objectives must be written. Skill is important; therefore, psychomotor objectives must be written. Attitudes and feelings are important; therefore, affective objectives must be written. Of course, **most objectives will contain or imply elements of two or all three of the domains**.

MAJOR CATEGORIES IN THE COGNITIVE DOMAIN

Evaluation:
Involves acts of decision-making, judging, or selecting based on criteria and rationale

Requires synthesis in order to evaluate

Synthesis:
Combines elements to form new entity from original one

Requires analysis in order to synthesize

Analysis:
Separates whole into its parts, until relationship among elements is clear

Requires ability to apply information in order to analyze

Application:
Uses information in a situation different from original learning context

Requires comprehension of information in order to apply in a new situation

Comprehension:
Interprets, translates, summarizes, or paraphrases given information

Requires knowledge in order to demonstrate comprehension

Knowledge:
Recognizes and recalls facts and specifics

SOURCE: Benjamin S. Bloom (Ed.), *Taxonomy of Educational Objectives, Handbook: Cognitive Domain* (New York, NY: David Mckay Company Inc., 1956).

MAJOR CATEGORIES IN THE PSYCHOMOTOR DOMAIN

Naturalization:
Completes one or more skills with ease and becomes automatic with limited physical or mental exertion

Articulation:
Combines more than one skill in sequence with harmony and consistency

Precision:
Reproduces a skill with accuracy, proportion, and exactness; usually performed independent of original source

Manipulation:
Performs skill according to instruction rather than observation

Imitation:
Observes skill and attempts to repeat it

Source: A. H. Dave as reported in Robert J. Armstrong et al., *Developing and Writing Behavioral Objectives* (Tucson, AZ: Educational Innovators Press, 1970)

MAJOR CATEGORIES IN THE AFFECTIVE DOMAIN

Characterizing:
Total behavior is consistent with values internalized

Organizing:
Committed to set of values as displayed by behavior

Valuing:
Displays behavior consistent with single belief or attitude in situations where he is not forced to comply or obey

Responding:
Complies to given expectations by attending or reacting to stimuli or phenomena; i.e., interests

Receiving:
Is aware of; passively attending to certain phenomena and stimuli; i.e., listening

SOURCE: David R. Krathwohl, Benjamin S. Bloom, and Bertram B. Masia, *Taxonomy of Educational Objectives: Handbook II: Affective Domain* (New York, NY: David McKay Company, Inc. 1964). Reprinted by permission of David McKay Company, Inc.

Optional Activity 2

For further information on the domains and the levels within each domain, you may wish to read Bloom, *Taxonomy of Educational Objectives, Handbook I: Cognitive Domain*; Krathwohl, *Taxonomy of Educational Objectives, Handbook II: Affective Domain*; and/or Armstrong, *Developing and Writing Behavioral Objectives*, pp. 24-37.

Optional Activity 3

You may wish to meet with your resource person or with peer(s) who are also taking this module to discuss the different domains. You could:

- Discuss specific performances from your own occupational area that would fit each domain.

- Review objectives in curriculum guides and categorize them by domain and by taxonomic level.

Activity 4

The following activity checks your comprehension of the material in the information sheet, Performance Objective Domains, pp. 34-41. Each of the following objectives is primarily cognitive (C), psychomotor (P), or affective (A). Read each performance objective, and indicate its primary domain by placing the appropriate letter (C, P, or A) in the blank to the left of the item.

DOMAIN IDENTIFICATION FORM

____ 1. Following a demonstration of techniques for stitching heavy materials, stitch given materials so that they will pass simulated inspection guidelines.

____ 2. Given samples of various legume seeds, identify each by name.

____ 3. Upon completion of the section on alternatives in business careers, demonstrate knowledge of the available career options.

____ 4. Define 90% of the editing symbols on a given list.

____ 5. On the assigned hospital ward, transfer doctors' orders to the appropriate forms for those orders. All forms must meet a satisfactory rating on the critical points outlined on the clinical evaluation form.

____ 6. Given ten lists of from 4 to 15 three-digit numbers, calculate totals for the lists on any of the four makes of adding machines found in the simulated office practice laboratory.

____ 7. Specify any missing or incomplete information on the five completed short-term loan contracts provided.

____ 8. In the clinical setting, demonstrate concern for apprehensive patients by:

- Answering call lights promptly.
- Staying with an apprehensive patient or seeing that someone will be present.
- Talking with the patient about the apprehension and answering questions about the unknown.
- Explaining all procedures before using them with patients.

____ 9. Calculate the missing value on 80% of a given list of Ohm's law problems that contain any two of the values for current, voltage, or resistance.

____ 10. Provided the necessary soil test data and necessary crop information, determine the kinds of nutrients to be applied to the soil to grow a crop.

____ 11. Using a soil survey report, determine the quantities of nutrients needed and outline the rationale for using previous crop and test information.

____ 12. When confronted with a safety hazard, demonstrate concern for safety practices by:

- Pointing out safety hazards to others.
- Turning off all machinery when it is not being used by self or others.
- Observing all caution signs.

____ 13. Given ten shafts with differing measurements, measure the diameter of each with a micrometer within ±.001 inch of the instructor's measurement.

____ 14. Compose a résumé that outlines your qualifications for a given job and contains all the components identified in the lesson on writing résumés.

____ 15. Change any cash register tape within two minutes so that the register is ready for tabulation.

____ 16. When confronted with a situation requiring the clarification of instruction, ask for clarification before proceeding.

____ 17. Given a written situation involving the adaptation of basic procedures, outline the method you would use to accomplish the task within the restrictions established.

____ 18. After reviewing a videotaped sales presentation, critique the presentation using the outline form provided. Your critique must match the model on all critical points identified.

____ 19. Grease all critical points outlined by the manufacturer on any car coming into the auto mechanics laboratory requiring routine maintenance.

____ 20. Identify the objectives on a given list as primarily cognitive, psychomotor, or affective.

NOTES

Feedback
5

Compare your written responses on the Domain Identification Form with the Model Identification Form given below. Your responses should exactly duplicate the model responses.

MODEL IDENTIFICATION FORM

1. **P**sychomotor
2. **C**ognitive
3. **C**ognitive
4. **C**ognitive
5. **P**sychomotor
6. **P**sychomotor
7. **C**ognitive
8. **A**ffective
9. **C**ognitive
10. **C**ognitive
11. **C**ognitive
12. **A**ffective
13. **P**sychomotor
14. **C**ognitive
15. **P**sychomotor
16. **A**ffective
17. **C**ognitive
18. **C**ognitive
19. **P**sychomotor
20. **C**ognitive

LEVEL OF PERFORMANCE: Your completed Domain Identification Form should have matched the model responses. If you missed an item, review the material in the information sheet, Performance Objective Domains, pp. 34-41, or check with your resource person.

Optional
Activity
6

You may wish to go through the list of objectives again, identifying the general taxonomic level of each objective. Refer to Samples 4, 5, and 6, or to the supplementary readings listed in this learning experience, if you need help. If you still have questions about the level(s) to which an objective belongs, check with your resource person.

OVERVIEW

Enabling Objective

Using resources that provide career/technical program content information, develop performance objectives in each of the learning domains that contain statements of performance, condition, and criterion.

Activity 1

You will be selecting resources in your occupational specialty that provide program, content information for all types of behaviors: cognitive, psychomotor, and affective.

Activity 2

You will be writing clearly stated performance objectives in each of the domains for the content you select.

Feedback 3

Your competency in developing clearly stated performance objectives in each of the domains will be evaluated by your resource person, using the Objectives Checklist, pp. 49-50.

Begin Learning Experience IV by selecting resources in your occupational specialty that will provide career/technical program content information for knowledge, skill, and attitude types of performances. Resources could include job/occupational analyses, curriculum guides, courses of study, textbooks, or task analyses. The resources you select should cover all domains. If you need assistance in finding resources, contact your resource person.

For the content you selected, write performance objectives in the cognitive, psychomotor, and affective domains. Write at least ten cognitive, five psychomotor, and five affective objectives, numbering each objective for easy reference during feedback. Be sure that:

- Each objective contains statements of performance, condition, and criterion.

- The performance is stated in action-oriented terms.

- The condition and criterion are realistic. When writing the cognitive objectives, include at least three objectives that call for higher-order thinking (i.e., more than mere recall).

After you have developed your performance objectives, arrange to have your resource person review and evaluate your objectives using the Objectives Checklist, pp. 49-50.

OBJECTIVES CHECKLIST

Directions:
Place an *X* in the YES or NO box to indicate whether all objectives met or did not meet each applicable criterion. For any objective(s) that did not meet a criterion, specify the number(s) of the objective(s) in the space provided for comments.

Name _____

Date _____

Resource Person _____

	YES	NO	COMMENTS

The cognitive objectives meet the following criteria:

1. The performance is specified.

2. The performance is stated in action-oriented terms.

3. The primary performance called for relates to the demonstration of knowledge.

4. The condition is specified.

5. The condition is realistic.

6. The criterion is specified.

7. The criterion is realistic.

8. The objective is measurable.

9. At least three objectives call for more than mere recall.

The psychomotor objectives meet the following criteria:

10. The performance is specified.

11. The performance is stated in action-oriented terms.

12. The primary performance called for relates to the demonstration of skill.

13. The condition is specified.

14. The condition is realistic.

15. The criterion is specified.

16. The criterion is realistic.

17. The objective is measurable.

The affective objectives meet the following criteria:

18. The performance is specified.

19. The performance is stated in action-oriented terms.

20. The primary performance called for relates to demonstration of attitudes/feelings.

21. The condition is specified.

22. The condition is realistic.

23. The criterion is specified.

24. The criterion is realistic.

25. The objective is measurable.

LEVEL OF PERFORMANCE: All items must receive **YES** responses. If any item receives a **NO** response, review the readings in previous learning experiences, pp. 8-11, 20-26, and 34-38, revise the objective(s) accordingly, or check with your resource person if necessary.

OVERVIEW

Sequence a given list of performance objectives.

You will be reading the information sheet, Sequencing Performance Objectives, pp. 52-54.

You will be logically sequencing the Performance Objectives: Getting a Job, p. 55.

You will be evaluating your competency in sequencing the performance objectives by comparing your sequence with the Model Sequences, p. 56.

For information on sequencing performance objectives, read the following information sheet:

SEQUENCING PERFORMANCE OBJECTIVES

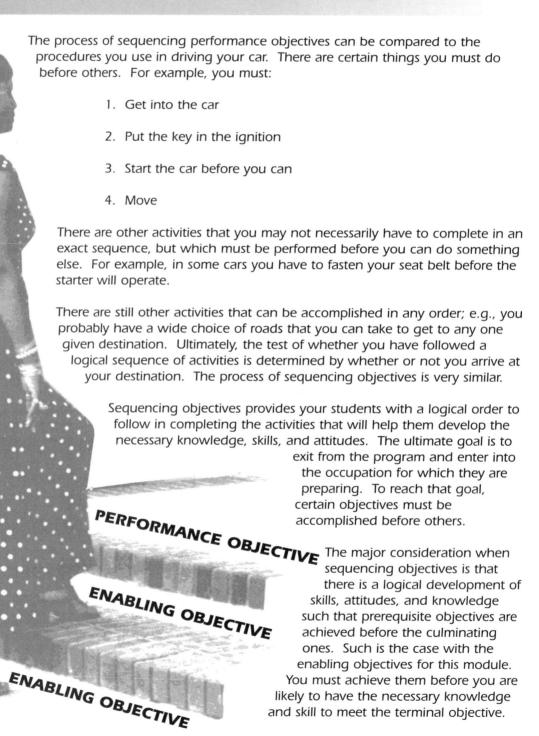

The process of sequencing performance objectives can be compared to the procedures you use in driving your car. There are certain things you must do before others. For example, you must:

1. Get into the car

2. Put the key in the ignition

3. Start the car before you can

4. Move

There are other activities that you may not necessarily have to complete in an exact sequence, but which must be performed before you can do something else. For example, in some cars you have to fasten your seat belt before the starter will operate.

There are still other activities that can be accomplished in any order; e.g., you probably have a wide choice of roads that you can take to get to any one given destination. Ultimately, the test of whether you have followed a logical sequence of activities is determined by whether or not you arrive at your destination. The process of sequencing objectives is very similar.

Sequencing objectives provides your students with a logical order to follow in completing the activities that will help them develop the necessary knowledge, skills, and attitudes. The ultimate goal is to exit from the program and enter into the occupation for which they are preparing. To reach that goal, certain objectives must be accomplished before others.

The major consideration when sequencing objectives is that there is a logical development of skills, attitudes, and knowledge such that prerequisite objectives are achieved before the culminating ones. Such is the case with the enabling objectives for this module. You must achieve them before you are likely to have the necessary knowledge and skill to meet the terminal objective.

The sequence chosen for this module assumes that:

- Students need general information about performance objectives (the rationale for writing them, how to differentiate between measurable/observable and vague objectives) before the other activities will be effective.

- Students need experience (practice) in analyzing simple objectives to determine if each contains statements of performance, condition, and criterion with out being concerned about the more complex task of dealing with objectives in the three different domains.

- Once able to recognize objectives that contain all components, students can be given information about, and practice in, writing clearly stated objectives in each of the domains.

The sequencing of performance objectives logically follows the task of having written them, and all of these experiences culminate in performance in an actual teaching situation. Thus, enabling objectives in this module are sequenced as follows:

1. Demonstrate knowledge of the rationale for developing performance objectives and the characteristics of properly stated objectives.

2. Identify the performance, condition, and criterion components for given performance objectives, and rewrite the objectives if necessary.

3. Indicate whether given objectives are primarily cognitive, psychomotor, or affective.

4. Write performance objectives within each domain.

5. Sequence objectives.

If the objectives had been sequenced as follows, can you tell what the rationale would have been?

1. Identify the performance, condition, and criteria components of given performance objectives.

2. Indicate whether given objectives are primarily cognitive, psychomotor, or affective.

3. Write performance objectives.

4. Write performance objectives within each domain.

5. Sequence objectives.

6. Develop a rationale for and differentiate between vague and measurable/observable objectives.

This is also a logical (although perhaps less desirable) sequence, one that moves from the *specific* (parts of an objective, how to write one) to the *general* (why write objectives, why be measurable/observable). Both sequences assume that:

- Students need knowledge about the components and domains of performance objectives before they can practice writing them.

- Practice should precede performance in the real world.

You may decide that your students need to achieve an objective that will catch their interest very early in the program, and sequence the objectives to achieve this. For example, you might sequence baking objectives before other food preparation objectives, on the assumption that many people like sweets and pastries better than vegetables.

Or you may decide that students need some overview of the total subject before you can proceed to specifics and, therefore, your first objective might cover a very broad area.

Or you may decide that your students need very early success within the program, and sequence some easily achieved and interesting objectives first before moving on to more difficult ones. In all cases, the assumption is that a certain sequence of performance objectives (e.g., simple to complex, known to unknown) makes sense in terms of students' needs and abilities.

Activity 2

The following activity checks your comprehension of the material in the information sheet, Sequencing Performance Objectives, pp. 52-54. Logically sequence the following performance objectives related to a unit on getting a job. Be prepared to explain why you sequenced the objectives as you did.

PERFORMANCE OBJECTIVES: Getting a Job

1. Explain to a prospective employer in a mock interview why s/he is qualified for the position. The instructor will evaluate the student's response, using the Interview Rating Checksheet.

2. Fill out a job application form appropriately, as judged by a representative of the business and/or industrial community.

3. Ask questions about benefits and opportunity for advancement and training in a mock interview situation. Evaluation will be made on the basis of peer and instructor feedback on the Interview Rating Checksheet.

4. Dress and groom for a job interview to meet acceptable criteria as developed by the instructor and a representative of the business and/or industrial community.

5. Develop a résumé to be used for a job application, that contains all necessary information as outlined in the sample résumé.

6. Write a letter accepting a position. The letter will be evaluated by the instructor using guidelines outlined in class.

7. Conduct yourself with poise (including manners and posture) in a mock-interview situation. Your performance will be evaluated by a panel of peers.

8. Write a letter of job application that meets minimum standards using the criteria listed on the Application Letter Checksheet.

Compare your completed sequence with the Model Sequences explained below. Your sequence need not exactly duplicate the model sequence(s); however, you should be able to justify any differences.

MODEL SEQUENCES

These objectives could be sequenced in several ways in view of the fact that we do not have data on the interests or abilities of the students taking the unit. Thus, we must look for a logical pattern in the objectives themselves. The objectives all seem to be at about the same level of difficulty or complexity and they do not divide into general and specific objectives.

They do divide, however, into:

- Objectives concerning the paperwork aspects of getting a job, and

- Objectives concerning behavior during an interview.

It would be necessary to have students begin by developing their own résumés, since they need to have a firm fix on their qualifications for employment before they can accomplish most of the other objectives. They could then work on the other paperwork objectives in any order, though a chronological sequence might make sense.

None of the *interview* objectives **must** be accomplished before any of the others—but they would, no doubt, occur in the same order as they would in an actual interview. The objective concerning poise would be accomplished **simultaneously** with the other interview objectives.

Thus, you would have a *paperwork* sequence (5-2-8-6, or 5-8-2-6) and a behavior sequence (4-1-3, with 7 being accomplished simultaneously with 1 and 3).

The objectives could, of course, be sequenced in a strictly *chronological* way, as illustrated below:

(5) Develop a résumé.

(2) Fill out a job application form.

(8) Write a letter of job application.

(4) Dress and groom for a job interview.

(1) Explain qualifications in a mock job interview and (7) conduct self with poise.

(3) Ask questions in a mock job interview and (7) conduct self with poise.

(6) Write acceptance or non-acceptance letter.

LEVEL OF PERFORMANCE: Your completed sequence need not have matched the model(s) exactly; however, you should be able to explain any differences. If your sequence differed from the model(s), arrange to meet with your resource person to justify the sequence you selected.

FINAL EXPERIENCE

Performance Objective

While working in an actual teaching situation,* develop performance objectives.

Activity 1

Develop performance objectives for a career/technical course you are responsible for teaching. This will include:

- Develop at least six of your own objectives or revise a list of existing objectives specified for a course.

- Include objectives in each of the learning domains: cognitive, psychomotor, and affective.

- Include objectives at various appropriate taxonomic levels.

- Ensure that each objective includes all three components: performance, condition, and criterion.

- Sequence the objectives.

Optional Activity 2

You are encouraged to use the Performance Assessment Form to evaluate your own work. It may also be helpful to ask peer(s) who are also taking this course to:

- Review your performance objectives to determine if they meet the criteria described in this module and listed on the Performance Assessment Form.

- Discuss ways to revise the objectives, if needed.

Feedback 3

After you have developed and sequenced your list of performance objectives, arrange to have your resource person review this list.

Your total competency will be assessed by your resource person, using the Performance Assessment Form, pp. 58-59.

Based upon the criteria specified in this assessment instrument, your resource person will determine whether you are competent in developing performance objectives.

---

* For a definition of an *actual teaching situation*, see the inside back cover.

PERFORMANCE ASSESSMENT FORM

Develop Performance Objectives (102-B)

Directions:
Indicate the level of the learner's accomplishment in writing clearly stated objectives by placing an *X* in the appropriate box under the Level of Performance heading. If, because of special circumstances, a performance component was not applicable, or impossible to execute, place an *X* in the N/A box.

Name _____

Date _____

Resource Person _____

Level of Performance

Components

	N/A	None	Poor	Fair	Good	Excellent
1. All objectives contained a statement of performance.	☐	☐	☐	☐	☐	☐
2. The performance statements contained an action verb.	☐	☐	☐	☐	☐	☐
3. The performance statements described the activity in which the student would be involved in sufficient detail to be understood.	☐	☐	☐	☐	☐	☐
4. All objectives contained stated or implied conditions.	☐	☐	☐	☐	☐	☐
5. The conditions were realistic in terms of the required performance.	☐	☐	☐	☐	☐	☐
6. All objectives specified criteria for achievement.	☐	☐	☐	☐	☐	☐
7. The criteria were realistic in terms of the required performance.	☐	☐	☐	☐	☐	☐
8. The criteria were realistic in terms of the conditions outlined.	☐	☐	☐	☐	☐	☐

Domains

	N/A	None	Poor	Fair	Good	Excellent
9. Cognitive domain objectives were included.	☐	☐	☐	☐	☐	☐
10. Cognitive objectives that required more than mere recall were included.	☐	☐	☐	☐	☐	☐
11. Psychomotor objectives were included.	☐	☐	☐	☐	☐	☐

	N/A	None	Poor	Fair	Good	Excellent
12. Psychomotor objectives were included that required more than mere imitation of the instructor.	☐	☐	☐	☐	☐	☐
13. Affective domain objectives were included.	☐	☐	☐	☐	☐	☐
14. The affective objectives were realistic in terms of occupational requirements.	☐	☐	☐	☐	☐	☐
15. The criteria for the affective objectives provided alternative ways for students to demonstrate the appropriate behaviors, feelings, and/or attitudes.	☐	☐	☐	☐	☐	☐

Sequencing

	N/A	None	Poor	Fair	Good	Excellent
16. The objectives were arranged in a logical sequence.	☐	☐	☐	☐	☐	☐
17. The sequence provided for the accomplishment of enabling objectives before terminal ones.	☐	☐	☐	☐	☐	☐
18. The sequence facilitated student accomplishment of the objectives.	☐	☐	☐	☐	☐	☐

LEVEL OF PERFORMANCE: All items must receive **N/A**, **GOOD**, or **EXCELLENT** responses. If any item receives a **NONE**, **POOR**, or **FAIR** response, the learner and resource person should meet to determine what additional activities the learner needs to complete in order to reach competency in the weak area(s).

NOTES

NOTES